ADMINISTRATIVE
and HUMAN RESOURCE
SOLUTIONS for
CONSTRUCTION PROJECTS

I0480290

ADMINISTRATIVE and HUMAN RESOURCE SOLUTIONS for CONSTRUCTION PROJECTS

Prem Vardhan

Notion Press

Old No. 38, New No. 6
McNichols Road, Chetpet
Chennai - 600 031

First Published by Notion Press 2016
Copyright © Prem Vardhan 2016
All Rights Reserved.

ISBN 978-1-945400-64-3

This book has been published with all efforts taken to make the material error-free after the consent of the author. However, the author and the publisher do not assume and hereby disclaim any liability to any party for any loss, damage, or disruption caused by errors or omissions, whether such errors or omissions result from negligence, accident, or any other cause.

No part of this book may be used, reproduced in any manner whatsoever without written permission from the author, except in the case of brief quotations embodied in critical articles and reviews.

TABLE OF CONTENTS

Introduction

Civil engineers have broadly four streams to choose for career building and employment:

Administrative and management jobs with government departments, very cozy, stable, and routine work.

- Design office of a consultant as a design engineer.
- Private companies around the town involved in the construction of buildings, town roads, and other civic amenity projects.
- Construction projects like roads, bridges, dams, airports, seaports, townships, and big industrial projects generally away from the city.

Major and mega construction projects away from the cities are full of innovations, challenges, and a good scope for a difficult, but respectable, rewarding, and enjoyable life for civil engineers, administrators, accountants, and a few engineers with expertise in mechanical, electrical, instrumentation and software engineering projects.

While one could see many good and interesting construction projects coming up and getting finished, at the same time, a few projects remain unfinished for a long time, due to public unrest and poor work, which are matters of concern and eyebrows are raised on the contractor just because social problems associated with the project were not handled properly.

It is well understood that contractually getting the land for the project is a job of the client, but if this is delayed, client engineer does not lose anything, but, on the contrary, contractor suffers due to delays and underutilization of resources, hence results in loss. Contractors with such attitudes should not venture into such difficult projects. Otherwise, they would land up in delays, bad faith, and prolonged arbitration proceedings.

This does not mean that entire job of the client is done by the contractor, but the contractor has to support with good liaising provided by his administrative team and monitory support in stray cases, with the knowledge and understanding of client engineer. Generally, he would reciprocate the gesture in some way or other.

The success of the project depends on the joint team effort of the project management and construction team. However, the project manager is the most important and key person, but he/she needs a good team of engineers, purchase officer, finance, accounts, and a very efficient administration and human resource manager, who all could work of their own under the guidance of the project manager. The primary responsibility of human resource manager is to assemble a good team for working on the project and simultaneously handle administrative problems related to the project.

The administrative and human resource manager has an important role in the project. His scope of work is generally underestimated. Ultimately, many senior officers have to support him, including the project manager neglecting their own work.

This book emphasizes on scope of work of administrative and human resource manager and problems, with solutions, for better understanding.

A construction project manager's role is to move from one place to another with his team members where nobody would want to go and live. When he makes the unlivable to livable, he gets ready to move to the next location, and this cycle continues throughout his life. In this process, every time the location changes, administration manager has to quickly arrange for reasonably good and comfortable temporary living facilities for the team as one of the first jobs.

During this journey, usually, his team members have to be friend with people of different walks of life, culture, source of living, and lifestyles including uncivilized tribes, smugglers and bootleggers who are difficult to deal with.

Procurement in-charge has to make new business friends and gain their trust and confidence for procurement of building materials, etc., for getting good services at reasonable prices and credit services from vendors logistically far away. It is difficult to pay every time at the time of purchase, due to logistic problems.

In order to deliver good result, they need to understand the new client and gain his confidence and get to know requirements.

Similarly, they also try to win over the consultants and gain their cooperation. In their new project, with a new consultant, there may be problems regarding approval of designs, method statements, and specifications of materials. When both contractor and consultant have not worked together and worked in different environments, they really need time to understand each other.

If a consultant lacks knowledge and experience, he becomes jittery and feels difficulty in accepting good proposals of construction methods and material proposed by contractor, which he has not handled earlier. The contractor has to slowly convince the consultant to accept the better methods of the contractor without hurting his ego and personality. This has to be done very tactfully with patience. They can even meet casually after office hours for better human relation building.

If a consultant is well-experienced and knowledgeable, he appreciates contractor's new suggestions, which he welcomes with an open mind, and the client gets best out of both of them the contractor and the consultant.

Employment of local workers is generally motivated with political reasons; hence, it is a challenge for HR manager to get the right people for doing the job without surrendering to local leaders. Or else job will have only politics and no work.

Further, team members have to undergo bitter experiences during construction like unrest between workers, unreasonable demands by local villagers and similar other problems. This has to be handled by project administrator during difficult situations, as the other side does not know whether their demands are reasonable or not. They begin with huge expectations and while understanding the situation they happily accept reasonable favors which may not be even 20% of original demand.

Project manager should not involve himself in the discussions since his decisions are final, while administrator could buy time on pretext of taking approval from his project manager.

All of these are done not just for financial gain, but also for satisfaction and pride. The team handles something difficult, not once, but again and again, throughout the life, in spite of many challenges.

Once, while working on the construction of a bridge, staff and officers usually got very tired by the evening, but they refreshed themselves with a boat ride, while coming home late in the evening, looking forward to the upcoming project and the sun that was setting beyond horizon. This was the only type of entertainment they had in addition to games and reading books. Television is recent and even now coverage is not available in remote places.

Their experiences are bit scary, but not exaggerated. The project is made successful with the combined efforts of a well-knitted team and every person in the team should have confidence and expertise in his field with a few assistants, especially in the initial stages, while others watch with anxiety. Yet, the new problems that might materialize will be addressed by them as and when the problems occur.

Project administrator and other human resource mobilization of employees with the right skills are very important functions for a successful project, and if good support is provided to the project manager, he could concentrate on other important issues of mobilization and execution of the project.

Works of HR along with the administration manager are divided into the following three sections:

- Social challenges.
- Industrial challenges.
- Human resources.

However, the whole team has to work as one unit to face these challenges under the guidance of administration manager and the project manager.

Social Challenges

Social challenges are quite risky for individual officers to deal with; hence it needs to be handled together by the team perceptively with a lot of courage and patience. The most essential factor is to understand the correct situation and the requirements of local people and bargain effectively, with convincing reasons, within the parameters that the contractor could afford. Once a verbal commitment is made, it becomes a binding and non-fulfillment of commitments is dangerous since these people are not adequately literate and word of mouth is very important. Once an agreement is made, they abide by it and expect the same from others.

Many projects do not take off the ground and are shelved, differed, or remain half-finished for a long time due to some reason or the other attributed to mistakes by the administration manager and his team.

It is an unspoken fact that the territories that are already developing fast, develop further faster, while undeveloped territories, next door, remain undeveloped. All important people in the society have some ambitions, and if the development is fast and many projects are in progress, all the ambitions are divided and focused to different projects. If there is only one project, everybody would try to show their importance and look for their share, which many times become unaffordable and confusing for the contractor. He takes negative decisions and tries to get out of the project or somehow finish with big compromises in quality. If a project is completed with low quality, it is mostly due to such hidden reasons, and contractor has to take all the blame.

In many underdeveloped or developing states and countries, pot holes in some particular roads are everlasting problem. Every year, a new maintenance contract is given for the road, at a premium price and money is spent for subjects other than repair of road, hence repair job is not done properly and is ready for repairs within a few months. This cycle continues with sufficient budget allocations every year. For this, nature is always blamed.

Some good companies refuse to compromise with quality, and then the project gets delayed, due to harassments to the contractor and claims are made, which get settled through the lengthy process of arbitration. But contractor may not venture next job with the same client.

A contractor intended to bid for a road project, and the news spread like a wild fire that a big company was bidding for this project, and their engineer was in town for a site visit. His phone number was picked up from hotel and all the people, connected directly or indirectly with the project, wanted to meet him to communicate their support for the project, as if contractor had already got the job. Contractor quoted very high rates to be safer in case of award of the contract. They were the second highest. Still there was an offer for negotiation, which was politely denied.

There are many tenders with clearly written in the document that the client is not bound to award the contract to the lowest bidder or any particular bidder. In such cases, tender is only an eye wash, and awards would go to the favored contractors.

A contract was given to a contractor with higher price, but still he did not finish in time, while the lowest bidder finished the other job for the same client on time with good quality.

TATA Group was trying to build a car factory in West Bengal, and even after spending a lot on infrastructure, they felt it was not viable, due to social and political constrains and walked out at a big loss gracefully.

Plenty of new or upgraded roads have some structure remain in dilapidated condition on the road alignment and not removed. This may be due to unsuccessful negotiations for the tiny piece of land with the owner, which might have failed due to reasons other than money.

Pre-tender site visit, besides technical challenges, must be studied/assessed for the following:

- Logistics
- Climate
- Possible social challenges
- Client's ability to pay in time

These are very important parts of pre-tender investigations, and are missed out sometimes due to ignorance.

Let us see some stories regarding how some challenges were managed after taking the contract in duress.

Gardh Mukhteshwar Road Bridge over River Ganges connecting Delhi and Uttar Pradesh around 1959

This bridge site was the place of hiding for a team of dacoits. They did not like any people moving in this area, which disturbed their privacy. They started creating problems by threatening workers of dire consequences if they did not go away. Further, on pay day, they would raid the camp at night and take away all the cash from workers and staff. They also placed some of their people to do labor jobs for the project, who hardly did any work. One day, while on duty, a relative of the chief dacoit was fishing in the river. Foreman Deshraj yelled at him for catching fish, instead of working, and slapped him.

Next day, the project manager received a letter from dacoits that Deshraj had attacked their relative, hence he should be handed over to them. It also said that on a particular day, they would send a vehicle to pick him up. All of them were tensed on the project, and many members of management volunteered to go in place of Deshraj to meet dacoits, including the project manager himself. Deshraj decided with lot of courage that he would go, since he was called, to have once-for-all resolutions to all the problems and avoid harassments on a daily basis. A jeep came in time, and he was taken away blind-folded. He carried a revolver, belonging to the project manager, hidden in the pocket, with an intension to kill a few dacoits before getting killed. After a long drive, he was taken to a big tree, where the chief was sitting with his associates on a small cot made of forest wood. Chief of dacoits welcomed Deshraj and asked him to sit comfortably, placing his revolver on table, stating that, "If we want to kill you, we will give you the first opportunity to shoot."

They treated him very well with fruits and milk. Once everybody was comfortable, they started the discussion, Deshraj very politely explained that this bridge was for their convenience and benefit, and still if they do not want, the construction people would go away, but later this bridge would be never built. After some discussions and assurance that the contractor would not inform police about their movements, they shook hands and become friends. He returned to the camp in the same jeep blind-folded later in the evening. Contractor completed the bridge without any further problem from them.

However, there was a beggar, with torn clothes, who came to their site with a dog. He lived there for a few months in very disgraceful condition. One would pass by without looking at him and always had covered the nose with a handkerchief, due to foul smell. He ate leftover food and always shared his food with his dog. Some workers, once in a while, would share their food with him. He would hardly speak, lived in open space, and slept in a small shelter at the site. He also used to sit near the group of workers discussing something, but people were not bothered about his presence, since he was considered mad. Nobody knew or understood where he came from.

The day after the bridge was completed and opened for public a big contingent of armed police came to the site, with a senior officer, who was shaved and well-dressed in a police uniform. As directed by the officer, police arrested all the dacoits. To everybody's surprise, the senior police officer was none other, the mad beggar.

Contractor and villagers gave him a big party in the evening and thanked for all the troubles he had gone through and suffered for so long for the good cause. Contractor had quietly informed police at appropriate level and this was kept as a secret. The dog was security to the police officer.

Saryu River Road Bridge at Ayodhya 1962

Contract for this bridge was awarded to a contractor. Ayodhya is a religious place with many innocent saints. Some people, for their personal motives, misled them and created problems. The government had fixed a temporary floating bridge on the river, and toll was collected for vehicles passing on to this bridge. The operators of this bridge were scared that they would close the toll after bridge is constructed and therefore they started creating problems. They even named their dogs after the name of the contractor.

When the first few trucks reached the site, unfortunately, a few branches of trees were broken, since they were lying low. A mob was quickly assembled to cut one hand of a driver, since he has broken branches of the trees. A group of administrative staff rushed to head priest and explained the situation. He came and resolved the issue amicably. They have to make friends with all sorts of people, when going to a new site. Even some of administrative team members of company consumed narcotics to give them company. If the head priest had not been in favor, then the situation would have been really worse.

Some mischievous people started spreading rumors that the contractor was making human sacrifices for the construction of bridge to please the river goddess. The operators tried various stunts but could not prove anybody missing. Contractor employed a big contingent of labor force from locals, which helped them to prove that they were not doing anything wrong. Such incidences stopped after one year when they saw the bridge was coming up really well without any major accidents or loss of life. These scarring situations are to be handled by executives having past experience to deal such situations

Road Bridge on river KOSI at Kursela, North Bihar 1965

This project site was on the banks of KOSI River, next to an existing railway bridge in Bihar. Nothing was available except poverty problems. Locals would rob for a few coins and even kill the person for the fear that he would inform the police. The contractor made the residential camp next to the site and engaged good security. Even to make a phone call, someone had to go fifty kilometers (km) by train to Katihar, the district headquarters. If someone wants to drive down, the whole day was needed. It was not safe to drive without proper escort, however, things have changed now.

Similarly, for buying anything personal, Katihar was only the nearest market. Once an engineer was returning from Katihar, by a late evening train, project administrator could not send the vehicle for pick-up to station at correct time. Since he was new to the site, he started walking. The railway station master stopped him, cleaned his own table, spread a newspaper and asked him to sleep until a vehicle came for pick-up.

Company on recommendations of administrative team gave some money as loan to a local person and he purchased goats and supplied mutton twice a week at an agreed price.

Another villager opened a shop at the site camp for daily needs.

They also prompted villagers to grow vegetables for them and installed a few water pumps in their fields.

They employed locals as work force, and many villagers, who were not getting even a square meal for a day, became prosperous.

Quickly, many of them became friends. Contractor completed the bridge and left a memorable relationship too.

Outer Harbor Project Visakhapatnam 1971–72

During this period (1971–72), Telangana movement was very strong. They wanted all the staff and workers from all the states, other than Andhra Pradesh, to go back to their natives and tried to stop the work by closing site gates, in protest of north Indians working in their project. All the staff and workers inside the gates remained at the site for three days and continued working. Other staff and workers in camp were not allowed to go to work and to replace workers at site for them to home and relax.

A native engineer, Venkateshwaran, along with him another engineer from north, decided to go home for a change, and Venkateshwaran said he would follow north Indian's jeep in his jeep for safety reasons. When he drove a small distance, a police constable asked for lift, to which north Indian happily obliged. Mob allowed his jeep to pass, may be because a constable was sitting in it. When Venkateshwaran jeep came, they stopped him, since he was native and still working while they were on strike, abused and put the jeep to fire and asked him to walk down to his house and not to return to work.

After a few days, people on strike were called for a meeting with all the leaders in contractor's office and showed that the strength of Telugu people was more than that of outsiders, and if one could get local experts to do the job and replace outsiders with permission of government, contractor did not have any problem. They could not arrange anybody confirming to specifications and strike was called off.

There was another problem due to a good number of local ladies, who used to befriend with officers and was a good conduit for employment of their relatives and friends for the project. Frequently, these officers would propose to employ a relative of those ladies who was very poor, and junior officers could not refuse. Contractor removed the senior-most officer involved in such activities, and then it stopped by itself.

Marmugao Port Project Goa 1973

This project started in mid-1973 with building site office and other ancillaries. In November, the project manager joined the project. Ten days later, he had a management meeting and it was stated that a particular section of workers may later become a source of problems, hence a decision was made to get rid of them, and instructions were given to the HR department to remove those workers.

Incidentally, the project manager had worked earlier with an engineer named Paul (name changed), who was now working on another nearby project in a different company. There was a rumor that Paul, along with union leader, was instrumental in killing his project manager a few months ago, due to some disputes with the worker's union.

A few days after removing that section of workers, somebody came to project manager stating that if he does not take back the workers, he would be killed and his family will not get even his dead body. The manager politely replied that he was not against them or any community and could also be checked with Mr. Paul with whom he has worked for a long time. The man replied that he would check and never came back.

But the same evening, the project manager drove alone to Paul's camp, for a surprise meet. They had a few drinks and a meal together. Project manager returned late in the night, without letting Paul know about the reason of the visit. And the job was done. If he had told reason of the visit in that meeting, Paul might have not helped, stating that he did not know anybody. They managed to complete the project without engaging that group of people and any union-related problems. One must think a few times before taking decisions, and once the decision is taken, try to manage it.

Arialoor cement project, Tamil Nadu 1975–76

After the project started, administration noticed that the area was full of limestone. Further, there was poverty, and food was available at very cheap rates, but without sufficient nutrition. Their staff, instead of eating in contributory mess, started eating the cheap food in restaurants and drinking dirty water. Within a few months, all fell sick. With some effort, administrator realized the cause of the illness and started giving food for free of cost and provided good drinking water to their entire work force and everything went back to normal. The job was completed very soon without any major sickness.

Soda ash plant for Gujarat Heavy Chemicals Ltd., Veraval 1986, in Gujarat

For this plant, a contract was given, to a contractor for building sea water intake and effluent disposal in deep sea. The contract was to be operated by all offshore activities with supplies through Veraval port. At that time, all the seaports of Gujarat were under the influence of a group of people. Nobody could do transportation of goods to ports in the region without concurrence of their chief. This job was sea-port based, and all the equipment and goods had to go to site through Veraval port. Project manager with his head HR went to their representative in Veraval before starting the job and sought his cooperation. He was sitting on a cot near his port field office in a hut, smoking local cigar, called beedi. He was delighted and felt honored by the visit to his small hut, he instantaneously removed dust from one of the rugs on a cot, offered to sit with a cup of tea and said, "You have given us honor with this visit, we do not want anything from you and your job will not have any problems from us. Instead, we will also support you in case of any problems in your project." Project administrator maintained good relationship with him. The job was done without any social problems or loss of money.

Site Grading for Steel Plant at Hazira, Gujarat 1988

First phase of Essar steel plant was on the banks of Tapti River. For the construction of the plant, substantial quality of fill material was required to fill the low-lying areas. Their engineer noticed plenty of dune sand heaps as natural deposits all over the fertile land. The land was left useless, due to this dune sand. Dune sand is not good for filling, especially when the ground water levels is high nor any vegetation grows on it, since it is porous, free of organics and liquid limit is very low.

They found solution for technical problems by providing extensive piles for the plant and stone columns at close spacing for stockpile areas and decided to carryout filling with dune sand. This was inevitable, as soil conditions in river bed were also very poor. These sand dunes might have been created by deposits by cyclonic heavy floods long ago. They discussed with villagers that they would remove the dune sand for free, so that the villagers could grow vegetables, etc., in their fields. It was difficult to convince the villagers, but they had no other alternative, since the land was useless to them and they could not get anything from the land in their lifetime. One landowner allowed them to try on a small patch and was amazed to see fertile soil under dune sand and that solved their immediate problem and removed all the dune sand even up to ten kilometers from the site. Both the construction people and the villagers had a winning situation and became friends soon.

Essar Oil Refinery at Vadinar, Gujarat Around 1992

Contractor started the job merely, with twenty percent land in hand, and rest under the process of accusation. They had an argument in the client office and some were of opinion that they should quietly start in a small way, without involving villagers in ground breaking ceremony. Other group argued that once they started the job, it could not be hidden from villagers, and instead of keeping distance, they should do it in the villagers' presence. Ultimately, the contractor called villagers and a priest from the same village, did a small prayer and started site grading and roads. They also employed locals from the village and gave earthwork contracts to influential people in the village. Those influential people helped them in land accusation to avoid idling of their own resources. The entire land required by them was with them before they needed it at a reasonable negotiated price. However, the final price of the land was slightly higher than expected.

Construction projects in Papua New Guinea 2010 onward in South Pacific Islands.

In 2010, ESSAR started construction operations in Papua New Guinea.

It is important to study the social and economic situations of any new site before starting the work. Further, this was an altogether different and new territory for contractor.

Papua New Guinea is a big island country in the South Pacific. It has vast mineral resources still unexploited very fertile land, very simple and good people, strong built and hard working.

Most of them have primary education, provided by Christian Missionaries, and are able to read and write, but the level of education in higher classes is quite low. Whatever job is taught to them; they learn it fast in a single attempt. They would continue doing the same job sincerely with full interest. Also, they wish to learn more and more, as opportunity is provided to them.

Tribals in the Komo village delighted to see a helicopter.

They are so contended and innocent that they do not have an idea how comfortably people live in rest of the planet. Everybody sleeps after having a square meal in the night.

The construction people had a stationary shop next to their office. When the truck full of stationary comes, everybody, including the manager, picks up the stationary on their heads to unload the truck, and shift stationary to the shop without considering his position.

Before project manager was ready to go to office, his driver used to wash the car daily meticulously and clean it completely (at least fifteen minutes prior to his journey).

Contractor observed the following basic qualities in people:

- They are strong and maintain good health.
- They are ready to do work hard.
- They are generally honest.
- They have basic education to read and write.
- They learn very fast.
- They have no requirements of their own.

Contractor changed his manpower policy and brought only engineers, office managers, high skilled workers and foremen from India.

Contractor employed locals and Indian construction workers in the ratio of 3:1, and Indians trained locals while working as their helpers. Very soon, the locals started working on their own and teaching their fellow workers, and eighty-five percent of the manpower strength of 800 workers were locals. Subsequently, contractor even had account assistants and clerical staff for office and stores. All this was not possible for project manager to achieve of his own without the support of good administrator.

What Did the Construction Company Get?

- They got about 700 workers locally without going through cumbersome visa rules and procedures. However, their overall efficiency in skillful jobs was low.
- They got workers at less than half of the Indians price.
- They saved camp facilities for over 700 workers.
- They got noticed, and important people started taking interest in their affairs.
- They started receiving invitations for new jobs.
- Local politicians were happy that so many families were served in their electorate, and simultaneously, they were also worried about retaining the construction workers in order to keep them employed and gave more jobs to the contractor.

What did the workers get?

- Instead of roaming on their streets, all of them became busy.
- They learnt new skills.
- They got an assured income every month, which was never experienced by them.
- They were supplied with proper clothes, hat and shoes.
- On late evenings working they received overtime payment and a good meal from four-star hotel was also provided to them according to their taste.

- After a few months, most people even constructed their own houses.
- The government organized viability classes for them in order to make them good and responsible citizens.
- Very soon, some of them had to pay income tax. Initially, the contractor staffs were worried how to convey this to them, but, they were happy, also honored that they were paying tax to the government.
- They were respected in the society.

The construction people were not able to increase their purchasing desire. However, they started living in-houses, which were made out of timber and steel roofing sheets, instead of thrash huts. Though it would take time for them to develop, it would be quite fast, since they had political awareness and desire for development.

Local citizens working on the projects also went to their villages and narrated all the happenings and their experiences at the site. This also helped them in increasing anxiety to make something better and new.

During day time, usually there would be a big crowd to notice what was happening at the site.

One afternoon, when project director was in the car with the Provincial Governor, the Governor asked the driver to buy three-roasted sweet potatoes from road side and kept it with him. After dropping project director at his home for lunch, the Governor went to attend another meeting, and on the way, he ate one sweet potato, and gave one to the driver, and kept the third one for his supper. It was not that he could not afford a lavish lunch at five-star hotels from his pocket. He could have also had lunch with us, as it was already lunch time, or had the next meeting as a meeting on lunch. In rest of the world, red carpets are laid for people of this status, but nothing works against simplicity and no desire.

All of their ministers, including the Prime Minister, moved freely in the country, mingling with people of all walks of life and drove their own vehicles.

Once the Governor was in the town, project workers stayed back at the site in the evening, hoping that the Governor would visit the site. The administrator went there. Since he was scared of the mob, he asked all of them to stay back and informed them that only two people can meet the Governor. They agreed and moved back, but when the Governor came to site, he himself walked to workers and had a friendly chat for a long time with all of them in their own language, and everybody was delighted and happy. He told us later that those were his boys and that they would never harm him. But, they also respected administrator too much and obeyed all his instructions.

Contractor could only support to some extent, and wish that such people, in Papua New Guinea and other parts of the world, grow faster and reach our living standards. It really hurt to see them in such a shape.

Contractor tried to increase the purchasing power of their workers, but the results were very slow. Unless the purchasing power of individuals was increased and a strong desire to have a better life arose among the nationals, the progress of the country development may not be fast. Still about seventy-five percent of the population is unemployed or under employed, but nobody slept with hunger. They managed with sweet potatoes, corn, pineapple, bananas, etc., grown in their garden/forest with least effort.

There are companies in Papua New Guinea and similar countries, who send almost all the money received in contract back home to their developed countries. Even eatables were imported from their parent country. This is a drain to the country's wealth. They employ practically no locals or contribute to the development of the community. There has to be a substantial local content in all the contracts.

OMAN AND OTHER GULF COUNTRIES

In 1973, Oman and other gulf countries–united–increased price for crude oil, and started building infrastructure, resulting in major development projects in their countries from loans and advances committed against the sale of crude oil from the developed countries, like the United States and Europe. These countries also brought the latest technology in infrastructure development with them. Gulf countries made rules that certain minimum strength of the work force has to be local citizens, and companies from other countries must have a local sponsor without which, a business license and visa for anybody would not be issued.

Outsiders were to pay just about 1.5–2% of their turnover to the local sponsor, in turn, the local sponsor used to help in business development, opening of bank accounts and other services as required by the contractor/businessman. It was an opportunity and means for development of local businessmen. They slowly started involving themselves in company affairs of all construction companies and related businesses by providing maximum support. Local businessmen even opened small construction companies and started supply of items for work and needs of foreigners. Still, there was a competition among locals to be a sponsor for good companies.

This gave opportunity for the development of many local entrepreneurs, which grew with this incentive. The government also encouraged growth with good education and bank credit facilities to the nationals. Today, they are self-sufficient in manpower, civics, education and administration. Now contractors need some experts and labor from other countries. It is worth noticing that now most of the gulf countries do not have locals to work as unskilled workers.

Initially, the contractors were getting watchmen from locals, and slowly the local people took driving and clerical jobs and grew very fast. They also sent their intelligent boys for higher education with the expenses borne by their countries and on return, the government gave them high posts with a few experts from overseas as assistants to guide and soon they took command of their department.

Still, major contracts are given to overseas contractors, but they understand the ground reality on social environment for their business and plan the human resources, according to rules of permitting only experts and labor from overseas.

Other undeveloped countries should take tips from these countries for the development of their country.

Industrial relations–
Challenges

Industrial relation building is a very important part of construction project management. It is necessary to build good relations with client, prospective clients, statuary authorities and the public. Without their support and cooperation, it is difficult to even exist on the project. It does not mean that one should bow down, but behavior should help in creating an atmosphere of coexistence, keeping consultants and owner on a slightly high platform.

As regarded by statuary authorities one needs to fulfill the official requirements and friendship with locals who generally place you on a much higher platform.

Mostly, all the major infrastructure projects of civil engineering are located in socially challenged areas. Our small help would improve their life, and one could expect lots of support from them in return.

One can help the local community in many ways without losing much.

The contractor was awarded a job to construct water canals near Baroda in Gujarat and went to a village named Dabohi, which was logistically suitable for their camp and office. Locals offered their houses for rental to the construction staff, and even built their office, according to their specifications and took nominal rent for usage.

A villager, after seeing their work, purchased an excavator and became an earthwork contractor to work with them. He hired an operator and was supervising the work himself to get maximum output. Slowly, they withdrew the supervisor from their contract, it was another saving factor. Ultimately, he became a big time contractor.

Once in a notorious area, near Mumbai, in 1977, the contractor was going to visit a new site for a sea-port at Navah. He was sleeping in the car while going to site and also while returning. He suddenly woke up. The car was stopped, and a villager, wearing just underwear and a big stick in hand was arguing with driver and scolding him. Contractor asked what the matter was. He turned to him and said that, "While this car was going to a nearby village, I asked for a lift, and the driver did not stop the car. So, now I intend to beat him."

The contractor asked him who he was. He replied "Everybody knows me. How come you do not know me."

The contractor replied, I am asking for your name? "My name is Prem, now what is your name?"

He said, "I am Pandu Seth, the biggest goon in the area."

Prem got down from the car, shook hand with him and advised the driver to give him a lift next time. He became very happy and became a good friend. Later, contractor purchased a truck on loan for him and instead of taking a helper for the task, he himself cleaned and washed the truck and returned their money before the due date. In the next election, he became a village head, after which he was sober and eventually became a good citizen, who was always properly dressed and presentable. He remembers contractor as his God Father. This showed how innocent he was, and how just a change in the environment made him so good, and even the whole family was changed along with him.

Currently, he lives in a bungalow and drives his own jeep, all hard-earned money.

In another case, there was a school teacher named Ram Thakur in the village near the same site. One day, around 1978, he came to them, wishing to do some business with them. First job he did was cutting the bushes by employing a few villagers and made a good profit. Hence, he got interested to do more work, and was obliged. Now, he is not only a famous and excellent national grade contractor, but has also opened a big educational complex for teaching graduations and post-graduation courses in many streams for students from poor backgrounds. It is difficult to find many good people who do not forget their roots.

In addition, the contractor gets fresh vegetables and fruits from the village at almost half the price of market rates.

Ladies from the contractor's office volunteered to teach children in their school for a few hours as a good time pass and as a service to the poor.

They also offered free medical services by allowing their doctor to attend serious cases in the village.

Once a while in the village, small donations were given for cultural programs.

Similarly, one can do a lot without spending much time and money to maintain a good relationship with the society and also its development for maintaining good harmony, which is very much necessary for a business and many major hurdles are avoided.

DO NOT INDULGE IN SOCIAL, RELIGIOUS AND POLITICAL AFFAIRS OF THE VILLAGE

While working in a new territory, it is very important to keep away from the weaknesses of the society. In India, a villager would work as an ordinary construction worker away from his village, but he will feel shy to do any work below a certain level to maintain his status in the village.

Social Affairs

It always looks good and interesting to mix with local society by participating in their community events and giving suggestions to improve the society. Every society has its own good and bad practices. These practices are not recent developments, but a few are deep-rooted for ages. For an outsider, to get indulged in social affairs up to certain levels of the suggestions may be tolerated, but unknowingly one tends to cross the thin border line, and then it sparks up and results in a conflict.

The contractor had a specialist at the site from London and became quite friendly with his engineers. One day, he said, "You bloody Indians!" This sparked an insult and he had to leave India in the next twenty-four hours.

Many a time, foreigners usually fell in love with young tribal girls, it works well up to a small limit, but in most of the cases, they have to leave the country in disguise or forcefully marry the tribal girl. Unfortunately, if they are already married, the life of their wives and kids becomes miserable, as these people would not let them go alone to any country. Anywhere, such things are not tolerated.

An Indian engineer fell in love with a Pilipino nurse in Oman, and she became pregnant. Project administrator reported this issue to the police. Police arrested both of them and put them under lockup. Then, the police approached the embassies of both countries and with the consent of both the embassies and respective parents, got them married and deported them straight from lockup.

A married Muslim engineer from north India fell in love with a Tamil Nadu Brahmin girl. The engineer had to run for his life and disappeared one night, sacrificing his permanent employment.

These incidences are matters of concern and gives inconvenience to everyone, and it disturbs the work, and in addition to all of this, the concerned company suffers by getting a bad reputation. It is necessary to keep everybody's brain occupied for maximum time, not only in the work, but also during relaxation in the best possible way while off duty.

Project Administrator should ensure the following:

Not employ young girls for camp maintenance.

Good living facilities with good hygiene, clean beds, toilets, hot water for bath and timely meals with different menu according to everybody's taste.

Nice garden with fresh air and outdoor games, like badminton, basketball, a basic gymnasium, good reading material, and some indoor games. There is no need for fancy table like tennis tables, etc., a table of required size made in the workshop is good enough.

Further, it is necessary for all the workers and staffs to go on vacation to their families according to the company's policies. This vacation should not be deferred for trivial reasons.

Mobile phones, with roaming facilities for limited talk time, are provided at the site, since the whole family waits for the day of his arrival and calling once in a day keeps everybody in the family content.

Often, if somebody was with a girlfriend and wife calls from home, he would talk to his wife first and the girlfriend gets depressed. If a telephone is provided, once in a day, he can talk to his family members, including wife, children, and parents, and stay away from evil deeds for his own welfare and family. He maintains a good and live memory to his family.

Once an engineer was in Oman, he received a telegram from his father in India that his brother was sick and requested him to come home for a few days if possible. He rushed back home in the first available flight and found that as if his brother was waiting for his arrival, as he expired within a few hours. It would have been bad if he had stayed back for some time, due to work.

Politics

A project manager should always stay away from local politics and support administrator to deal diligently.

While starting a new project in the Jawaharlal Nehru Port Trust (JNPT) Port near Mumbai, which was a very notorious place, the project manager was approached by a known political leader who said he would select unskilled manpower for the project and would be responsible for the conduct of the workers selected by him or his team, which would obviously give him a political mileage. Project manager agreed and fixed a meeting in the village school with villagers and the politician. When the project manager with his team reached the village, police stopped him, advising him not to enter the village, due to security reasons. Project manager walked in the village with his team, followed by the police, after discussions and agreement with a police officer. It is noteworthy that the police were not an escort to him, but just followed him. Impression on villagers is different in both of these situations and first impression is very important.

To his surprise, the leader of the opposite party was sitting on the dais, introduced himself as the real controller of village affairs and offered the same proposal to the project manager. Project manager made it very clear to him, and public assembled in the school, that he did not want to get involved in local politics and sought the support of all the people in the village for construction of the project.

However, due to internal fight between the two political parties, this project was not smooth and a unit of armed police was posted at the site, but the company and its project manager always remained neutral, and hence survived the project.

Essar was the first to enter the notorious Raigardh District in 1976 and did many projects until 1990 successfully, just because they were neutral between two warring political parties. They discussed only business and nothing else and leaders of both parties were friends. No major strike, except minor disturbances, happened at the site for the entire working period.

In Papua New Guinea, two cousins were politically arch rivals, sitting in ministerial positions. The contractors were friendly with one brother, which the other one did not like and created some minor problems. They resolved those problems by themselves without involving their friend. Slowly, the other brother also became a friend and started supporting them in their business.

They clearly told everybody that they do not wish to get involved in any politics and it was appreciated.

Religion

As a matter of fact, ultimately, all religions converge in one, but there is so much diversity between the religions, and often, officers favor their own religion or support a particular religion. In such circumstances, this differentiation is clearly visible to others, and very soon, different groups get formed and lead to internal conflicts.

Workers' attention gets diverted, and instead of working productively, they spend time in gossiping and planning as to how to make the other group look inferior. This is a serious damage to the team spirit of the work force. Project, progress and quality of work become second priority and project administration starts slipping resulting in delays and loss.

A project manager can be successful and have a control on the workforce only when he is neutral and common to all. While taking decisions on personal matters, no consideration, other than behavior and performance, should influence his decision-making process.

In Oman, a section of Muslims was cooking in general mess and eating beef quietly. On getting reports, administrator called a meeting of Muslims and Hindus. Hindus do not eat beef. And Muslims do not eat pork. One group proposed in the meeting that they were willing to compromise if both beef and pork were allowed/not allowed. The meeting finished in ten minutes amicably with a decision that beef and pork both would not be allowed in the kitchen.

For a job in Indonesia, they had two kitchens, one for Indonesians and another for the Indians, since their eating habits were different.

In Papua New Guinea, pork is the national food. Contractor could not avoid cooking in the kitchen and everybody, including Muslims, accepted, however, cooks took care that if any non-vegetarian dish, chicken, beef and pork were cooked, it was cooked in separate vessels. There were many strict vegetarians also, and all of them ate together on the same table from the same kitchen and servicing staff, caring about everybody's sentiments.

The contractor once went to Bandar Abbas, Iran, for a project, and initially, their staff stayed in a hotel. Hotel restaurant was mixing beef, even in vegetable soup, according to local taste. They explained to the hotel manager that Indian vegetarians could not eat this type of food. Since there was no alternative, they expressed their willingness to depute their own cook, free of cost to the hotel, in their kitchen to cook vegetarian food. Hotel manager felt sorry for what happened and said, "You are our guests, and it is our duty to take proper care of you." And, from the same evening, the Iranian hotel cooks prepared special delicious vegetarian food for them for the entire period of stay in that hotel.

CLIENT–CONTRACTOR RELATIONSHIP

The contractor should not talk about his personal relationship with the client while discussing business with him. It is seen invariably that client might keep on asking for favors by way of changes and improvements, which contractor would not able to refuse.

Contractor should not take unnecessary favors by always telling that he is losing on contract and prepare undue claims. To be fair, client should get the finished project on time at the right quality as per contract specifications, and contractor should get his justifiable payments on time including the payments for extra works done on the contract.

Client visit to project site

The client is the end user of the property or facility built by the contractor. His visits to project site should always be welcomed and facilitations with flowers, if possible, and a cup of tea.

There should not be very heavy arrangements for his welcome, unless his visit would be useful for other new projects or any reason other than this contract.

Too much expensive greetings sometimes give negative signals, resulting in demands and favors by the client. The client starts thinking contractor is making good money on the project or cheating by diverting attention.

It is always good to provide a safety helmet and safety shoes to the client before entering the site.

It is advisable to inform the consultant as early as possible about the proposed visit for his presence and client giving direct instructions to the consultant about variations, changes and consultant noting any other good or adverse comments from the client.

The client always has the right to visit the project site, but as a protocol, he should inform consultant and the contractor in advance of his intent to visit the site.

If proper representative of the contractor is not available at the site, security can refuse entry of the client, basically due to security and identification reasons. If he still insists, the security chief and project engineer available at the site should accompany him and politely deny any information sought by the client, since they are not authorized to deal directly with the client.

The contractor is the custodian of site and responsible for upkeep and safety of everybody at the site.

Generally, these visits are with the following objectives:
- See the progress of the work.
- Quality of work and finish.
- Cleanliness at the project site.
- Any items of works forgotten in original scope and any new ideas that might crop up during the visit, requiring variations and additional works.

As a preparation for visit, following documents should be handy at a clean place, with a table and a few chairs arranged accordingly by the contractor:
- Full set of drawings.
- Status of billing with a summary of money received till date.

- Project time schedule and status of work progress as on date.
- Statement of proposed variations waiting approvals.
- Some stationary for making sketches, etc., during discussions.
- Any other problems, preferably written down as points for discussions.

During this visit, client may give some instructions. These instructions, including visit notes, should be properly recorded and sent to the consultant for approvals with the copy to client.

Correspondence and Discussions with Client

Correspondence with the client depends on his involvement in the project. It is always better to prepare a correspondence matrix at very start of the project among the client, the consultant, and the contractor.

All decisions regarding variations in the project are ultimately made by consultants after discussions with the client. It is better to request client that this decision has time and cost implications, hence, it is better that the instructions are given through the consultant, who can make a cost estimate and put it up to client for the approval.

Just by knowing that this decision will have time and cost implications, the client would jump, "WHAT ARE THE IMPLICATIONS?"

To this, one has to reply politely, "Sir we would work out and let you know."

At least 20% of instructions if not more the client would instantaneously withdraw and give a decision that he does not want that change. It may be annoying, but it is good to be clear that there is a limit for getting something for free. Otherwise, one would keep on doing variation jobs, and both consultant and client would ask for more and more. When one asks for money, initially, the decision would be delayed, and ultimately, one may be lucky if contractor could get just costs after prolonged wait.

In any case, one should have a balanced approach and discussions. The client and consultant should not feel that contractor is claim-oriented. There is a difference between a claim and variations. A claim is asking for something extra for doing the agreed scope of work, due to any reasons like escalation in costs, delays in decision-making, physical conditions are not the same as defined in contract, etc., while variations are just asking for money for something extra to the scope in contract. Sometimes, interpretation of contract on the subject is treated as claim, instead of variation. In such cases, the ambiguity should be resolved before doing this work.

Always two separate files should be maintained for claims and variations, and correspondence should also be numbered in separate series.

The competence of the project manager and his team in maintaining good industrial relations is judged by noticing that a client gives a repeat order or not, without going out of way to please the client and his consultant.

Consultant-contractor Relationship

On a construction project, consultant for the project has following responsibilities to the client, irrespective of who has designed the project.

- Check and release construction drawings for the project for execution.
- Check and approve shop drawings and bar bending schedules submitted by the contractor.
- Check and approve the time schedule of the project.
- Check and approve a method statement for the project.
- Check and retain safe custody of bank guarantees and insurance policies obtained and submitted by the contractor after his own approvals communicated to client and contractor.
- Check and approve quality assurance and safety manuals for the project.
- Check and approve resources mobilization schedule, including manpower and construction equipment.
- Check and approve qualifications and relevant experience of the project manager of the contractor.
- Check and approve material specifications to be used for the project, including the source of procurement.
- Check and approve baseline survey of the project.
- Check and approve actual construction work is carried out as per specifications, method statement, safety manuals, and quality assurance plans, with quality controls, as specified in approved quality assurance plan.

- Overseeing of work is carried out in a cordial atmosphere and he has right to remove anybody from the site who do not work properly or who indulge in unwanted activities. He should give advice in writing to the project manager with reasons for taking such actions. However, the project manager if not in agreement with the consultant, he may appeal to him first with assurance that such acts would not be repeated at the project site. If consultant does not agree, project manager can escalate the issue to client.
- Check work progress bills submitted by contractor and submit it to the owner for payment.
- If there is any discrepancy found in work progress bills, it should be communicated to contractor, and after agreement with contractor, any adjustments required are done and corrected bills are sent to owner for payment.
- Check and approve variation in consultation with owner.
- Check contractor's claims and submit his unbiased opinion to owner and process to the satisfaction of himself, owner and contractor.
- Close the contract after finishing it.
- Observe structural behavior and proper usage of the completed project during defect liability period and advise contractor to rectify the defects if any.
- In case of misuse or accidents, due to no fault of a contractor, get them rectified/repaired by the contractor as a variation on payment.

From the above statements, one should understand the importance of consultant, and it is important that requisite status is provided to the consultant, and sometimes it is a misunderstanding that if project managers are friendly with the client, the consultant is not important and could be neglected.

On a multi-storied building, the contractor prepared a sample ceiling and showed it to the client, and then the client approved it. Hence false ceiling was considered unnecessary. It was a lump-sum contract. Contractor started finishing the ceiling, and it was looking really good.

After some time, the consultant visited site and demanded false ceiling, since it was necessary to absorb noise, and the rooms get better acoustics with false ceiling. Contractor said, "Ok, we will do false ceiling at an extra cost."

When the bill for false ceiling was submitted to consultant, he refused to pay, since the cost of false ceiling was included in the price of the project in the contract. The client could not help the contractor.

In Essar oil refinery project, the consultant rejected the soil at the site for filling in low areas and recommended imported fill, tenders were called, and contract was to be awarded to the lowest bidding contractor at a very high price, he was to remove all the bad soil and take them away from the site, dispose in areas arranged by the contractor and replace with good soil brought from outside conforming to specifications.

The matter was referred to the sister company, Essar Projects, who proved to the consultant that only top soil was not fit for filling, and good for green belt, and the rest conformed to the specifications if handled with care. Essar Projects was awarded the contract at one-third of the usual price and finished it before time. However, Essar Projects had a tough time with the consultant during execution. If any other bidding contractor did proper investigations and bid the contract by giving discounts for alternative methods, he would have won the contract and made good profits.

On a new project, contractor should provide an office with telephone and internet facility for usage at the site by the consultant.

It is always advisable that when consultant goes on rounds to the site, a contractor's senior representative should accompany him and discuss about various issues to be resolved and try to resolve without entering in correspondence and involving the client. Client should only be formally advised by the consultant of changes and seek approvals before proceeding implementation of the proposed changed scope of work.

In case of any problems or modifications in the opinion of contractor, it is better to discuss them first in the consultant's office for better understanding and try to resolve amicably.

A good work in a friendly atmosphere, with little and minor compromises, is always appreciated.

Suppliers-contractor Relationship

Around 30–40% of the cost of a project is cost of supplies of materials, construction equipment spares and oils & lubricants, and it is important to keep the supplies moving into the project according to requirements with least scarcity. In cases of scarcity of even one item that is required for the project, the project suffers and activities on the project need to be re-oriented/re-scheduled to avoid or reduce its impact on the progress of the project and idling of resources.

Whatever good planning is done, there will be anxious moments, due to shortage of something or other, due to various reasons–including logistics, shortage in the market– due to short supplies, quality issues, delays in releasing purchase orders and cash flow problems.

How frequently and seriously such problems arise depends on the overall management of the project, and it is difficult to clearly assign the responsibility to one person or division.

It is vital to know that it is always, and especially in such circumstances, the relationship with the suppliers plays an important role. If the supplier trusts the management, he could help in a long way to resolve the problem or even avoid the problem by keeping extra inventories for emergencies.

Usually, good suppliers take even extra pain to get your material by air at their cost.

Once when a contractor in Mumbai needed a small part of an echo sounder the survey equipment used in marine works, which hardly breaks the supplier of equipment in Singapore sent with a passenger on the next flight to India with ten pieces of that part next day morning, and collected by the engineer in Mumbai on airport on his arrival.

In Visakhapatnam outer harbor project, a contractor purchased about ten heavy duty excavators from the manufacturing company of such equipment. Within a few months, the main gear of the excavators started breaking one after the other. The excavator's manufacturer immediately deputed his senior engineer at the site along with enough spares and saw to it that the work was least affected, due to this problem and rectified all the equipment.

For a large project, many suppliers maintain inventories in their own warehouses for a few bulk materials, saving on the contractor's warehousing costs and reducing strains on cash flow. The specifications have to be provided and rough monthly intake of the material should be indicated so that the supplier can supply the materials at an agreed fixed price. However, for such facility, the supplier needs firm commitments from the purchaser and even provide bulk purchase discounts.

The contractors generally buy contract items like rebars, cement, timber, lubricants, and supplier maintains inventory at standard rates. They also provide an approximate takeoff schedule and advise variations in requirements, a few days in advance.

Nobody sits on a pile of money and does business. It is a chain of commitments, and everybody must keep a buffer in the bank for the possible delay in payments from his client to fulfill his commitments down the line. Still if there is a delay, it is better to inform the creditor in advance of a possible delay, in order to make it convenient for him to make his own arrangements, instead of waiting for the contractor's payment. It is bad if there are reminders for payment from suppliers.

Similarly, the supplier should have honest dealings in supply of the right quality at a right price and in time. All purchasers look for good and reliable suppliers on a long-term basis, but at the same time, continuously check in the market to see whether he is supplying material at a reasonable price and quality.

Some suppliers take the buyer for granted and start charging high prices. This is risky and whenever the purchaser realizes that the supplier is not fair to him, he would stop dealing business with him and go to another supplier.

Simultaneously, the purchaser should always have his own checks of quality, quantity and price of materials to make supplier understand that this client is vigilant and cannot be cheated. Good buyers keep two or three suppliers for each item of purchase and distribute the work on the basis of performance of the suppliers. Any lethargy on this subject, would create problems in the long run and loss to the company.

CONTRACTOR'S RELATIONSHIP WITH BANKS

For any business to exist and grow, relationship with banks has to be good. Business needs money to perform and grow. This money can be provided by financial intuitions and banks on the basis of track record in financial dealing and fulfilling commitments of businessman, the contractor.

Banks take a risk by providing bank guarantees to the contractor's client and suppliers on behalf of the contractor, and in case of failure by the contractor in fulfilling his commitments, bank would pay the agreed amount to the beneficiary, irrespective of whether the contractor has money in the bank or not as a commitment.

Further, as per his requirements for the project, bank provides cash credits to the contractor. Invariably, the moment cash credit facility is sanctioned by the bank, there is a sudden spur on spending, as if the money is gifted and not to be returned, and finish the sanctioned amounts in a short period. The bank officials are not fools, they would observe the outflow, and patiently fulfill their commitments, but the next time, they would be cautious and may even ask for outflow plans with justifications.

A company got another contract with 20% of contract value as unsecured advance payment, and no performance bank guarantees were required to be given to the client, in fact, this was a favor to the contractor, since the client trusted the contractor and gave this repeat order. This job could be done with positive cash flow throughout the contract period, and the project did not need any financial support.

Accounts manager in head office went to bank and asked for hefty facilities against this contract, and as a rule, gave a copy of the agreement with client for this contract to the bank. The senior officer of the bank not only refused to give the requested facilities, but also called the project director from overseas to his office and scolded him for cheating like behavior of finance manager. In addition, utilization of existing facilities was made more difficult. The contractor terminated the accountant to avoid such mistakes, but lost face to the banker.

Big business establishments maintain good trust by fulfilling commitments on time with banks, and with the bank's support venture into new businesses. Hence, commitments with banks are to be fulfilled by any means.

A contractor commits to the client through bank and insurance company's commitments of payments on his behalf to the extent of more than twice the value of contract, in case of non-performance or failure.

This is hardly understood by many project managers and his senior associates, the responsibility and the trust the contractor has bestowed on them on performance of the project. This is often taken casually by the project managers and his senior associates, who find faults with others in head office to save themselves in case of problems. Similarly, head office executives should be careful in giving instructions to the project manager.

The contractors will be happy if some senior executives of projects would start counting the commitments made by contractor by trusting them and try to prove worthy of their confidence.

COMMUNITY AFFAIRS

Construction administrator has to deal with a large number of people from the local community for a good performance on his contract. His work affects the local community in the following ways:

- All of a sudden, a large number of outsiders arrive to live for a short time and use their infrastructure.
- Community is eager and concerned: up to what extent and why they should provide support to the contractor?
- How much their presence would disturb their peaceful living?
- What do they need from the society?
- What would be the character of these people and how would they behave?
- What languages do they speak?
- What do they eat?
- How do they live?

In this photograph, when the contractor's representative arrives at a remote location, the village people become upset, as their peace would be disturbed, their land would be taken away, and they would have other social problems, hence villagers would not allow the contractor to enter into the village. One man is shouting, and all the others are listening.

In the second photograph, the leader talks to the project manager and team asks for their benefits and the project manager assures that there would be no interferences in their social affairs, especially, contractor would not take away their land by force. He makes commitments along with his administrator with instructions to the administrator to fulfill all the commitments he has made.

In the third photograph, they are convinced, happy, shake hands, and stand together with contractor's project manager posing for a group photo–with smiling faces.

It took about two hours for them to convince the people for allowing them to enter into the project site and start mobilization amicably.

It is the responsibility of the contractor to abide with all the decisions and commitments made by his representative in the village.

Generally, the following are expected from the contractor:
- Provide employment and training to the villagers as required by the contractor.
- Contractor would not employ workers from a village not having friendly relations with this village without the consent of the village chief.
- Keep the site clean.
- Ensure safety of villagers and their property by avoiding accidents.

- Do not interfere with villagers' social issues.
- Consume products from the village, like vegetables, fruits, etc.
- Drivers should be careful while driving around the village.
- The contractor will not forcefully occupy any land, unless all the formalities of land acquisition are completed.

HUMAN RESOURCES

Contractor needs well-educated, experienced, and dedicated personnel to execute contract. It is not only difficult, but also impossible to have one hundred percent success in selecting an ideal team for any project, and it is the responsibility of the project manager and his human resource department to select a team as efficient as possible. They should also retain to extent possible the inefficient and underproductive colleagues with them and get maximum possible output out of them.

Long ago, the contractor's engineers were not tolerating inefficient employees and removed them from company within a few months of their joining. One day, the Chairman of company called them and said that he was fed up of employing new people, since they kept on sacking them. He said that if twenty percent of fresh recruits are good, it is an achievement.

Training employees to work according to our requirements should be learnt by our engineers and by all reasonable means, retain good employees. Company had ultimately had a very good number of employees joining in the early days of their career, and retired from the company after working for a long time.

Some of the team members could be over qualified and experienced. This often poses a different type of problems. They are never content, and if their job profile is not according to their status, they always crib and tend to move out on getting a better job. They should be given proper assignments soonest either on the project or other project of the company.

Estimation of Manpower Requirement

First, based on the tender estimates and his own experiences, project manager makes rough estimate of overall manpower requirement into three categories, namely:

- Senior management
- Middle-level management
- Workers for the project

Advise administration and human resources departments to plan out project establishment.

He also prepares a list of the manpower required to start the project in different categories and gives it to HR team for their initial planning and arranging the necessary manpower to start the job.

He adds a senior engineer to the team to provide technical support.

This team goes to the site and starts looking for local talent to work on the project under the guidance of senior engineer.

Often the project manager also makes short visits to site to have a real feel of the project.

The team also scouts for employees, which could be transferred from other projects.

Most ideally, the work should be started with local manpower and equipment hired locally for a short period, and other resources could be add-ons progressively, so that there is some progress at the project site, and problems start surfacing early and are resolved before smooth operations and full mobilization is completed. Further, if work starts early, it helps with cash in flow to the project.

It is never advisable to wait for full mobilization of resources before the start of work.

Even the Japanese, the most-efficient planners, also start a project in stages. An advanced team visits the town to start some activity locally while their own resources are in transit.

On the first major road contract, a contractor spent three months in office in planning for procurement of construction equipment and manpower, and then went to site to notice that most of the land was not acquired by the client as per contract, and even for cutting a tree, they needed to undergo time-consuming approval process. They could not stop or delay new equipment from arriving at the site, since advances were paid with confirmed orders. Project started with frustration and finished after three years with the same frustration, because even by then, a few patches of land could not be acquired by the client.

Simultaneously, a detailed estimate is prepared for the requirement of manpower with their qualifications and experiences related to the project.

- First scope of work with major quantities of different items of work is worked out.
- Time schedule for execution of the project, with histogram of different activities, is prepared.
- Histogram is an estimated graph of quantities of work to be executed per week or per month for different items of work plotted on time, and unit quantity scales for each group requiring similar manpower. Theoretical histogram is usually a zigzag curve. Quantities of work

done per week or per month are adjusted in the time schedule to get a smooth parabolic curve separately for each group of activities with the consent of the project manager. All the activities should start and slowly increase, go to an optimum progress level, and then toward end, close fast, but not abruptly to provide adequate provision for unforeseen reasons for problems and delays in closing any activity.

- Quantity surveyor, planning engineer and human resource manager should sit together and diligently decide number of man-days required for executing each unit of these activities.
- The planning engineer and human resource manager together would upload these unit man-days on the activity histograms of each activity and get histograms for manpower of different trades.
- Support services, like logistics, camp operations, transport for the workers, security, safety, sickness and first aid, holidays and vacations, travel, time keeping, accounts, clerical jobs, water, and power, etc., are further activities that are not covered in the engineer's planning schedule, and manpower for these activities are further assessed by administrator and planning engineer.
- Summary of workers is prepared and submitted to senior management for review.

Supervision and Management Staff Estimation

Human resource manager and other senior teammates work out the management structure and number of supervision and management staff, based on the following:

- Construction and engineering challenges expected in the project.

- Extent of design engineering to be done at the site.
- Work to be done by direct workers or subcontractors and extent of subcontracting.
- Supervision of staff for direct workers is generally divided as one supervisor for twenty workers and one senior manager for seven assistant managers.
- It is always desirable that from peon to project manager, everybody should have direct responsibilities and work should be distributed to utilize everybody's full capacity by giving multiple responsibilities to individual executives, depending on the work load. A few combinations could be made as under:

  + Planning, estimation and billing
  + Marketing, estimating and tendering
  + Finance, accounts and audit
  + Human resources, industrial relations and administration
  + Safety, first aid and time keeping

- A few people, like junior engineers and foremen, doing similar jobs should have their job description properly identified and separated.
- Everybody should have just one boss for reporting, i.e., a worker reports only to his foreman or supervisor and foreman reports to his engineer. Anybody reporting to more than one person will always create confusion.
- If all the building materials and equipment are available locally, then procurement team would be small. The team would be bigger if procurement is within the country, and still bigger if procurement is from overseas. In case of overseas procurement, work on logistics is increased and more qualified and experienced procurement

manager may be required. Staff required for logistics and camp management is also added.

It is usually not advisable to have social challenges as the singular responsibility of administrative manager, since it is a big and difficult job. It should be handled together as a team, and follow-up should be a responsibility of administration manager under guidance of project manager and/or a teammate assigned by the project manager.

Generally, a certain percentage of total manpower has to be taken locally as a condition of contract, and even otherwise, a serious attempt should be made to employ locals on a project even at the cost of some training. This is economical as it saves money on camp, travel and social problems, besides establishing goodwill with locals.

For workers and staff, care should be taken that employees are taken as a mix of all religions and many possible territories.

In some cases, if contractor himself is from a particular state and/or religion, he prefers to have most of the people from his own territory. This works very well and more dedication by employees is visible if a contractor is directly involved in the project or is having a very efficient project manager of his choice. But, in such cases, the choice of executives also becomes limited to this territory, and employees outside the group find difficulty to continue for long.

Job Description for Individual Categories

Once the final template of new recruitments, along with job description for each category and skill, is prepared, HR team proceeds for recruitment.

Job description note should include following:

- Designation
- Qualifications
- Minimum experience in the relevant field
- Age group
- Reporting pattern
- Nature of the job and expectations from employee
- Location of project and related logistics
- Living constrain factors, like entertainments, possibility of family accommodation and schooling facility with standard of education
- Leave, overtime and rate of overtime if payable and other benefits, like leave travel assistance, etc.
- Salary bracket to be offered with details of allowances
- Maximum allowable joining period

Employment Contracts

Draft employment contracts are prepared for different categories, since they are different in many ways, like reporting pattern, perquisite factors, terms of employment, notice period, probation period, etc., generally according to standard guidelines of the company. These draft employment contracts are to be cleared by the project manager and approved by the head of human resources of the organization.

Recruitments

All the documents, as described below, are sent by project human resource head to the central recruitment department of the company. They would scrutinize and make necessary changes according to company's policy and recruit the required personnel through their own recruitment channels with following guidelines.

- Number of employees to be recruited for each category
- Time schedule for reporting at the site
- Job descriptions
- Draft contract agreements

Central recruiting team may recommend necessary changes for the consent of the project HR head, who, in turn, brief the project manager and if there are any special concerns, inform to head office for their consideration.

The central recruitment team would shortlist a few candidates to be personally interviewed by human resource manager and a technical representative This list would also include in-house candidates. this team has rights to select or reject any or all the candidates and process is continued till full complement of manpower is selected.

As a matter of policy, on a project site, chiefs of accounts, human resources, safety, quality, and Management Information System (MIS) should functionally report to their respective heads in head office and only administratively report to the project manager. Hence, these function heads in head office usually select their representatives and send them to the site with consent of project manager.

This does not mean that they are equal or above the project manager. They have to maintain good discipline and work efficiently in a transparent manner, taking responsibility of their department and work in the best interest of the project in consultation and guidance of project manager, knowing very well that ultimately the project manager is singularly responsible for performance and profitability of contract. They should also mark copy of all the correspondences with head office to the project manager.

It happens many a time that accounts officer is not in agreement with project manager, for certain expenses, he goes to project manager and shares his point of view, but if project manager still feels his decision is correct, due to any reason, but is not able to convince accounts officer, his instructions in writing prevails and accounts officer still pays and he may send the deliberations to the head office for their information and with this, his responsibility is over. Same principle is applicable to all the disciplines.

This is good for everybody in the following ways:

- A good transparency is maintained between project and head offices on all the key matters.
- Head office could suggest improvements and measures to be taken.
- Head office is also accountable for loss and profits for some extent. They just cannot say that we do not know anything.
- Function heads become more accountable and efficient, instead of toeing the line of project manager and making him responsible for all the incidents that had gone wrong at the site. Hence, the function heads are expected to put up right recommendations to project manager and if necessary, copy to head office.
- Since all the correspondence with head office is copied to project manager, any mischievous deeds or wrong reporting are avoided.

Site HR head has the responsibility to coordinate the progress of recruitment with head office, including providing any support required by head office and periodically report the progress to project manager.

Project manager can interfere if the progress of recruitment is not found satisfactory.

MOBILIZATION AT THE SITE

While recruitment is in progress in head office, HR and administration departments at site arrange suitable accommodation for new joiners. If camp is not ready, accommodations in rented houses or hotels are arranged hotels being the last choice and restricted for shorter duration.

If the project duration is more than two years, or good rented accommodation is not available, a suitable plot of land is selected for building a temporary camp with good connectivity to the nearest road, water, power facilities, and a place away from the swamp, etc., suitable for healthy and hygienic living. Total cost of accommodation should not be more than one year's rental of houses.

If necessary, it should be discussed with other executives at the site and decided on priorities of facilities required first, especially kitchen and sanitation, and then the accommodation as per mobilization of manpower schedules.

Basic amenities required are hygienic toilet, fresh towel for bath, a good sleep, and nourishing food on time.

A few cases of solving initial problems:

The contractors went to a new project site about a bit away from nearest town, and the town also did not have adequate basic facilities. Initially, their staff used to bring bread, butter, and vegetables for a salad for lunch and had a proper meal at night in the town after returning from site.

Project Manager went to a nearby petrol pump, hired a room in the warehouse, and made a makeshift officecum-kitchen. They also bought a kerosene stove and a few utensils, and started cooking hot and hygienic lunch at the site, and then shifted to the camp progressively, as it was getting ready.

In 1980, an engineer went to Fahud oil fields of Oman for a contract. Their workers and staff used to leave camp at 6.00 am, with packed lunch, and returned to camp around 7.30 pm. Lunch was a proper meal, prepared in kitchen from 4.00 am onwards, but they ate the food around 1.00 pm, that was lying hot in lunch boxes for almost eight hours. He started calling their vehicles back to the camp that was 80–110 km away and sent fresh food for lunch. Everybody was happy, including cooks, and the productivity increased.

In Komo air field in Papua New Guinea, they hired a good four-star resort about forty kilometers from the site for the first four months and kept their workers and staff in the resort, air lifting one and all by a helicopter everyday morning and evening from resort to site and back. Even though this was very expensive, they had to do it until accommodation at the site being built by these workmen and was ready. And the work started, simultaneously on time without any delay. There was not even a proper road to the site for four-wheeler vehicles. Trucks had to change tires for every 2,000 km.

Simultaneously, this section of road was upgraded and started using the road for manpower transport and diverted the helicopter to other important duties.

All these decisions are usually proposed by the HR and Admin head to project manager, and implemented by his team after approval.

It is noteworthy that during the mobilization time, number of executives is few and an all-around mobilization is to be carried out. In such circumstances, everybody has to take his charge to himself without depending on others, hence very capable HR Executive is sent to site first. He gets applauses or abuses for a good or bad job done, which has to be used, as it is till the end of the project. Every contractor has a few people very good in this work, and all the project managers request one of these at least for the first few months of their project.

CAMP FACILITIES AND LIVING CONDITIONS

Camp accommodation is generally built in the form of barracks as follows:

- First plinth is built about 1-m high with stones or brick masonry for all the outer walls of the barracks.
- This is filled with a good soil and well compacted.
- If necessary, a 20-cm soling is provided on this fill.
- A 0.25–0.5-mm thick HDPE film is spread on the top of soling/fill.
- A 75–100-mm thick concrete screed is placed with a good trowel finish on the entire area, except toilets and bathroom areas. This screed would serve as floor for the accommodation.
- On top of this screed, the building is erected with walls in either of the following material:
  + The interlocking pre-fabricated panels are sandwiched with thin steel plates on both sides with a 50–75-mm thick polythene foam or similar material injected between the plates.
  + Hardwood of 50 × 75-mm timber frame is covered on both sides with a thin 5-mm size waterproof ply wood on outer walls and 3-mm size on inside of walls nailed and painted. In case of frequent rains, all the outside face of the building should be corrugated steel sheets.
  + Some other decent, durable, and inexpensive panels.

+ Roof is generally asbestos corrugated or steel corrugated sheets on steel or timber trusses and 3-mm thick plywood false ceiling on a timber frame.
- Toilets and bathrooms should have waterproof walls with tiles on floors and walls with flushing toilets. Hot water facilities for bathing, exhaust fan and window for ventilation are provided.

For senior managers, independent room, attached toilets are provided.

Next level would be twin sharing rooms with attached toilet.

Workers will be provided about ten in each big hall with common ablution unit, and a dedicated cupboard for each worker by the side of his bed.

Proper air circulation with fans, exhaust fans, and split air conditioners as approved.

Separate kitchen, laundry and dining facilities for officers and workers. Dining facility is generally used for celebrations and meetings. Cooking in rooms is discouraged, otherwise camp has to be upgraded for upkeep of hygiene, waste food management and fire safety.

Other facilities include gym, table tennis, TV room etc.

All the barracks would have doors on both sides, connected with all-weather durable roads. Dispensary and camp office would be in a central place.

There should not be any water-logging anywhere, and proper drainage should be provided.

A badminton court, car park, smoking area, sit outs, etc., are also provided with good illumination in the camp for night movements and sufficient fire extinguishers at all the strategic locations should also be provided.

Fencing should also be done with car parking within fenced areas.

Food

For project workers, heavy breakfast, light lunch, and good dinner are recommended. Everybody has to exert a lot on projects, and therefore they should eat good food properly.

If central kitchen is provided, quality of food is controlled, and people do not spend their spare time, which they hardly get for going to the market to buy groceries and cooking food. Sometimes, if they are much tired, they feel lazy, and sleep without taking food.

These kitchens are generally contributory every employee contributes for food expenses, and company provides cooks, utensils, etc. A committee of three or four employees are planned to have an eye on expenses and maintain accounts. The committee members keep changing on rotational basis.

On a particular construction project, most of the employees lived at the site, and the project manager and a few others having school-going children lived in a town away from the site office. Lunch was prepared in the office pantry for everybody. Suppliers and other business associates were happy to visit the office, since they need not struggle for food, as it would be served hot and delicious. Especially, when people came in an angry mood, half of their anger used to subside after eating. Administration used to make sure of serving them food before starting discussions.

Entertainments

It is a saying that a human brain never sleeps and when tired, the best way for the brain and body to relax is to change the subject and divert to another mode of thinking and actions. Therefore, a change of mind after returning to camp after a day's hard work is very much necessary. Mostly, there are no family and kids in camp and they are away in native places. Hence, some entertainment and diversion of mind is much required. Very important for this diversion of mind, they should not runaway to club or market etc. After a change of clothes.

When everybody returns to camp after a days' work, a cup of hot tea or coffee, with some hot, light snacks, is always welcomed. After this break, some would go to bath, or play outdoor games, like badminton, gym or watch TV, and sleep after dinner.

Especially, when employees are returning to camp after a long night shift, they are in a hurry to sleep as well as feel hungry, and if there is a delay in this facility, many times, it sparks off a big annoyance among them and an unpleasant atmosphere is created. This has to be avoided.

The following facilities are recommended, but it is generally based on choice of employees:
- Magazines
- Newspaper
- Carom board, table tennis or chess boards–any one of them
- Television
- Badminton, basketball, etc., any other game
- Gym and walking track
- Light music
- Small well-laid garden to sit out in the fresh air to relax and some casual discussions
- A comfortable smoking area

Medical and First Aid

A dispensary at camp, with a male nurse, is a basic requirement and is not expensive. It can be supported either of the following ways:

- Arrangement with a prominent doctor in nursing home in town. Male nurse takes all the patients to him daily in a particular time slot. Doctor gives medicines, since he is on actuals basis and ultimately becomes expensive and inconvenient. For small illness, he would generally escalate and give plenty of medicines.
- Either male nurse is capable to handle general cases or put a junior doctor in the dispensary. In addition, a senior doctor comes two or three days a week in the evening and provides only consultations for a fixed fee.
- It is advisable to have an own doctor in the camp, well-experienced and having a tie-up with major hospitals only to refer major sicknesses and accident cases.
- Selection of an alternative depends on the nature and size of job and logistics.

Accidents and their Managements

Life is very precious, and nothing at project site could be more expensive than a human life. Hence, full precautionary efforts are necessary to avoid accidents, and in case of an accident happening, the affected person, irrespective of his status, must get the quickest and the best possible medical treatment, and at the same time, a panic-stricken situation should not be created.

Once during a construction project, a senior employee had a severe heart attack in his house during night time, he was rushed to the hospital and so much panic was created by the family, the doctor also got influenced and decided for do an early surgery, but could not control the situation at the time of open heart surgery, due to increase in blood pressure of the employee (this was told to us) and ultimately the patient died after surgery.

In Fahud, oil fields in Oman, 1980, a pick-up had three summersaults due to high speed late in the evening, and twelve people got injured. They were all shifted to the first aid clinic. The male nurse took two hours to examine and provide first aid to all of them, briefed the base hospital, and decided to shift at the earliest two patients for surgery and balance could wait till morning.

As per directives of base hospital, air ambulance came after four hours and during this time the male nurse prepared two patients ready for surgery as directed by base hospital. The four hours' time between first aid and transport by air ambulance in the night was spent for stabilizing the patients and making them ready for surgery, keeping in the first aid post. The male nurse kept them under his care, instead of immediately shifting by air ambulance. In the meantime, operation theaters were also made ready with doctors in the base hospital waiting for patients.

Above all, male nurse decided on his own about who needed immediate transfer to the base hospital. The others went by a regular aircraft, special flight to base hospital next day early morning. Everybody returned from hospital after treatments in good health.

One should neither be in a hurry nor, take it easy, and should take decisions with a balanced mind in consultation with a medical team.

ON-JOB TRAINING

If one takes a small quantity of soft wet clay, it can be molded the way one wants but it is difficult to mold the same quantity of dry clay. It would not mold, but rather break. Similarly, it is difficult to train to an old executive. For company's growth, one should take young executive trainees and train them according to requirements. This is applicable to all the categories of employees. Further, it is much cheaper to take young boys and girls and train them while working on lesser salary with full of enthusiasm and ultimately retain the good for further training. It is the responsibility of human resource department to select young boys and girls, with basic knowledge/education, having potential and interest to learn and grow, for all the departments. Suitable training atmosphere for on-job training and monitor their progress in consultation with their trainers is necessary and recorded.

On the job training is provided as under:

- When a fresh employee joins, there is a small discussion about the scope of the project and a slot of responsibility, which could be provided according to his wish and education.
- A few days are given for understanding the job and change of his duty if necessary.
- It is always appreciated if the employee prepares a set of questions, otherwise training is provided step-by-step to do the job, and it is monitored.
- Trainee is now given a specific task to perform under guidance of his trainer

- It depends on their grasping power – few of them learnt early, while others took a little more time.
- A little later, they start working without a guide and start taking decisions, which should be encouraged.
- The biggest satisfaction and pride for a trainer is knowing that his trainee can work better than him.
- At the same time, the trainee should always respect his trainer and take his guidance when problems arise.
- Once an engineer was required to carry out rock-blasting operations, which he had no idea about, and was an altogether a different technology and expertise for him. He was chosen, since management thought that he would learn fast, and was deputed under a quarry superintendent, who was freshly hired for the project. Soon, he learnt everything for routine job and was given an independent charge. He thought that he has become equal to his boss. For one of his mistakes, the superintendent was called and scolded, but he straightway said that the engineer does not report to him. The engineer lost his independence and had to report to superintendent until he finished the project.
- But that engineer, an old employee and considered an asset to the company, had learnt this technology and company started getting more contracts on the basis of his experience.
- In addition to these, classroom trainings for about a week duration are also provided to executives about two to three times a year by experts on the subjects.

Further, there should be casual discussions to encourage employees to grow, and they should also feel that someone is following their progress. Human resource executives should also impress and convince the young ones of rewards for good training and improvement, which cannot be in the form of quick promotions and increments. There are organizational procedures for such rewards. A company invests on providing opportunity to learn at company's own risk and costs, which itself is a big award, and they have to wait until such time that the company gets convinced that a particular employee could be promoted.

Normally, a big section of employees leaves the company, when they feel that they have learnt enough. There is no point of holding them back, as they will not stay for long. One does not lose anything, as they have worked and justified their costs of staying and working till then. If someone is not good, senior executive may get rid of him as early as his present assignment is finished and work-wise satisfy that he or she is not the right one to maintain for a long-term.

Senior executives, good at their work, do not change employments easily unless some unavoidable circumstances make them to change. Hence, it is difficult to get good trained executives.

Further, on joining a new organization, there are only two options: either this executive changes himself or change the organization to his style of working, both are difficult. Hence, he makes a few changes before settling down somewhere and if not, returns back to the old organization.

A few keep on rolling the whole life and that is also an art of working. Changing jobs after three to four years after working in one organization, when there is no real productivity or responsibility taken. They are usually experts in shifting responsibilities. Always be careful and alert and convey to your superior your observations. Sometimes, it is annoying, but still, it is good for organization. Same time, juniors should be careful of damages they could do by shifting responsibilities.

Still, when somebody joins an organization, as a senior manager or a director, the status itself provides a certain freedom to act, and management expects accountability and commitments from him. So long as he fulfills his commitments, there would be an opportunity for more and bigger commitments, and this is how one can establish himself in the organization, grow and enjoy the assignments and carrier.

It is difficult to get experienced people, which is a fact, hence provide training to executives from ranks and retain them, is good for stabilized organizational growth, and hence on-job training is necessary and it works. If good people leave the organization, there has to be something wrong somewhere and this is the responsibility of human resource department to identify the problem and clear the misunderstandings by counseling at both the ends as required. Still, if he or she leaves, record the reasons for leaving properly in the exit interview to enable easy return in the future.

Periodical Performance Reviews

Increments and promotions are given to all employees once in a year on the basis of their performances, evaluated by their reporting executives and their recommendations. Generally, senior executives make their recommendations on the basis of their impression, which may not be correct and it happens that a favored employee rises fast, and a performing employee is left behind.

Further, there should not be a policy of providing promotions on the time scale and, if provided in the HR management system, it should be implemented without any exception. It must be understood and clarified clearly to all the employees at the time of recruitment that performance review is a competitive exercise and not just individual performance.

It happens that on a good performing a project, everybody has performed very well and appraisal is conducted on the basis of the best out of the best. While on a non-performing or much easier project with lower grade of skills, selection is done on the basis of better out of good. This creates a disparity in promotions among the employees across the company. There has to be equal recognition and marks provided for a category of employees across the group/ organization.

There should be categorization of the projects on level of skills, logistics, and overall performance of the projects and adequate and justifiable weightage to be given in performance appraisal of employees, based on the project they are working to judge all employees on different projects at the same platform.

It is observed everywhere that everybody prefers a cozy job or to work under an influential project manager, giving quick promotions. This practice should be discouraged. If awards are given on merits and competence across the organization, employees would run for challenging assignments and rise fast with more quality and respectable life. Further, complacent project managers would get up, rise on their feet and perform even better.

Many performance measuring tools have been developed, and the evaluations are done in a systematic procedure, and these procedures are very effective if all the concerned executives give their quality time and importance to it.

Some of these systems are quite complicated and difficult to understand without an in-depth reading and effort to understand, which a boss finds it difficult to concentrate, due to other pressing commitments. It is therefore important that someone from head office visits all major establishments and takes a session for a few hours for all the executives together to explain the procedures of evaluation.

Further, when the head of the human resource evaluation system gets changed, and he or she introduces his or her own system, which is altogether different, once again the whole system goes for a toss. These systems are important for the organization and should be selected carefully to be user friendly and productive, and once tested and approved, they should not be changed, just because the operating executive in HR department is changed.

Usually, project manager requests head office to send an expert to explain the new system, this request is turned down by stating that project HR should have competence to explain. Well, the request is because the project HR head himself does not understand the system. Ultimately, project executives do what they could do and send reports, which are evaluated by a computer, and results could be well understood, and such situations must be avoided.

Town Hall Meetings

On a project site, executives and workers come to work and live together from different walks of life, territories and working cultures. Occasional meetings are necessary between management and employees to thrash out the following:

- Any suggestions to improve quality, safety and productivity.
- Any inconveniences in general, regarding living conditions, food and suggestions for improvement.
- Any dissatisfaction or complaints with management and their resolutions.
- Any improvements suggested in working culture.
- Safety measures taken on projects are adequate or further beefing up is required.
- Transport, recreation, etc.
- Any social or political problems.
- A brief talk given by the project manager on company affairs.
- Any other item requiring the attention of management and workers.

These meetings are called town hall meetings and generally are conducted once in every three months. In these meetings, the senior members of the project management at the site conduct open discussions with all the workers and officers regarding various issues and resolve them in a cordial atmosphere. Generally, these meetings are held on an off day and concluded with a nice dinner, with everybody served on the same table. Dining tables and discussions groups should have a fair representation of all the levels. Record notes of discussions are prepared and circulated.

Routine Works of HR and Administration Departments
Administrative Jobs
- Statuary compliances
- Labor laws implementation
- Immigration and visa formalities
- Travel
- Guest management
- Vigilance, security, and reporting

Human Resource Department
- Attendance and time sheets including overtime payment on the basis of actual productive working and not considered as bonus given by the bosses
- Payroll preparation
- Provident fund, insurances and gratuity of employees, management
- Leave records
- Conveyance for workers
- Placements on new projects on the completion of the project

Routine jobs, as discussed, are manageable by a junior executive with a few helpers for small or mid-sized projects and for large projects, two separate executives for HR and administration could be provided.

A well-experienced executive or a group of executives are necessary to handle and take decisions related to social, industrial and human resource problems, which are very important to be resolved in a short period. Any sort of lingering or delay on the part of management make affairs more complicated and demands from opposite sides keep on increasing very fast, and usually becomes unmanageable, and eventually, the project suffers.

In a head office, there are usually separate senior executives in-charges for these functions, hence one group or person dealing with all these affairs on the project becomes an administrative problem, but this should not a very big problem. One man can report to different section heads, only related to their jurisdiction.

Simultaneously, it is not advisable to dump all these problems on the project manager, who in the majority of cases, does handle the issues, as there is no other alternative for him, and if not successful, the project manager is changed, which is another mistake and it escalates to shelve the project after changing a few project managers.

One can name the department the way one likes, but a few trusted administrative or HR junior executives are groomed by the organization to handle such problems under efficient project managers, and as they grow and arrive at the routine job, additional responsibility of procurement or accounts, etc., could be given to keep them fully occupied and justify their salary.

Shelving of projects after partial mobilization or half-way of finishing construction is very common in big industrial houses and government.

This affects the company's reputation, and leads to a big cash loss. Number and frequency of such projects are big. It would be improper to disclose names of such projects.

However, the example of TATA's car factory in Bengal can be cited, since it is well-known and really a very big loss, which only organization, like TATA, could have managed to bear.

BLOG

Administrative and Human Resource Functions are the key supports to a project manager. They are responsible to make or break the project. Here we have tried to elaborate their job profile and challenges with suggestions for solving the problems. A few true success stories of working and behavior of these executives in different selected difficult circumstances are also added.

An effort has been made to guide executives responsible for these functions, by providing necessary knowledge and detailed discussions on various small but important issues to carry out their work in most challenging work environments smilingly and successfully with full confidence but never to fail.

Alternative

Human resource and Admiration function are the key support to the project manager. They aide the project manager, in achieving milestones in the journey of successfully completion of the project. This book is well illustrated with on the job case studies, highlighting challenges faced in different work environment, the problems and their solutions.

An effort has been made to provide a written guide to the executives, responsible for the various administrative and Human Resource Functions. Books read out detailed discussions on various small but very important issues which if neglected, can create obstacles for work force and hence slowing down the project. The three important Ps for a HR Executive to remember are:

Productive

Performance

Positive motivating environment, with a smile.

www.ingramcontent.com/pod-product-compliance
Lightning Source LLC
Chambersburg PA
CBHW071222220526
45468CB00002B/701